Rigby Literacy
Collections 5
Middle Primary

Contents

WHALE SH

Greg Pyers

Gentle Giants

Whale sharks are the world's biggest fish. Adult sharks may be as long as 14 metres and weigh as much as 10 tonnes. Whale sharks may be huge, but they are also among the most harmless animals in the sea. In fact, at places such as Ningaloo Reef, off the north-west coast of Australia, tourists in scuba gear can swim right beside these animals. The whale sharks seem untroubled by this attention and sometimes even swim up to investigate the divers.

Diet

Unlike large carnivorous sharks, such as great whites and tiger sharks, whale sharks do not feed on large prey, such as seals or turtles. Rather, whale sharks feed on the tiniest of marine animals. These include very small, shrimp-like animals called krill, and even smaller plants and animals called plankton. Krill and plankton form dense clouds in the water, made up of millions upon millions of individual animals.

Feeding

A whale shark eats krill and plankton by swimming along near the surface of the water with its huge mouth wide open. Whole swarms of krill and plankton are drawn into the shark's gaping mouth, along with many hundreds of litres of seawater, of course.

As the shark swims, usually at around one or two kilometres an hour, the seawater passes from the shark's mouth to its gills and out through its gill slits. Gill slits are vertical openings just behind the shark's head.

As the water passes through the gills, sieve-like structures called gill-rakers trap the krill and plankton, which are then swallowed.

ARKS

Life Cycle of the Whale Shark

Surprisingly little is known about the life cycle of the whale shark. For example, until very recently, it was not known whether whale sharks lay eggs or gave birth to live young.

However, the discovery of 300 unborn shark pups inside a dead female shark has cleared up this mystery. Scientists have estimated that whale sharks may live to be a hundred years old.

Whale sharks do not stay in one area all year. The 250 or so that visit Ningaloo Reef arrive in March and leave in June. Where they come from and where they go when they leave is still not known.

In a day, a single whale shark may eat 50 kilograms or more of krill and plankton.

Whale sharks usually feed at night or late in the afternoon.

Where Whale Sharks Live

Whale sharks are found in warm seas all around the world. They usually swim near the surface either close to the shore or well out to sea. Whale sharks are attracted to places where cool deep water meets warm surface water, and plankton grows in abundance.

Judo Medals Up for Grabs!

They say it's like a game of physical chess—a sport that takes both brains and brawn for an athlete to be successful. Judo demands mental precision and intense speed and agility from its players.

Judo, according to those members of the Australian national squad bidding for selection in the 2000 Olympic Games, is the ultimate duel between two athletes' bodies and minds. In Japanese, the word "judo" means gentle. But watch the athletes train or go into combat and the word gentle doesn't come to mind!

Judo was founded by Professor Jigaro Kano in 1882 as a tamer alternative to the more dangerous martial art of "jujitsu" which was used by the samurai warriors of ancient Japan. When judo was introduced at the Tokyo Olympic Games in 1964, everyone thought the Japanese would win all the medals. They almost did!

A Dutchman named Anton Geesink won gold in the open event. Women's judo was introduced in the Barcelona 1992 Olympic Games.

For the first time, Judo athletes in the 2000 Olympic Games will wear coloured judo suits, called "judogis" (one will wear blue, one will wear white), instead of the traditional white judogis.

An Olympic match begins with a ceremonial bow. When the referee gives the command "hajme" (which means begin fighting), men have five minutes and women have four minutes to score a single point or an "ippon", and win the contest. An ippon is scored when a player is thrown onto their back and pinned down for thirty seconds or when a player is strangled or arm-locked into submission. If neither athlete has scored, the referee and judge decide who is the winner.

Australia used to be the easy team to beat in judo competition —a team which could never threaten leading competitors from Europe and Asia. But that has changed. Australian judo— particularly the women's team—is on the rise and regarded as a worthy challenger in international competition. The men's ranks also continue to grow, with several young athletes showing their potential on the world stage.

In 2000, 400 competitors from several nations will contest the seven events for men and seven for women. The Japanese, Korean and French contestants are the ones to beat.

As the host nation, Australia will send its largest team to the Sydney Olympics, entering athletes in all fourteen events.

Carly Dixon, a member of the Australian Judo team (left), competes against an opponent.

On the dairy

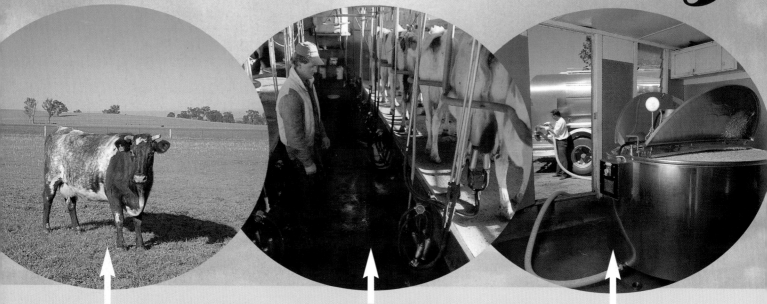

At the farm: Dairy cows are cows that are farmed for their milk. Dairy cows are kept on dairy farms. These farms are usually in areas where there is a lot of rain and the grass grows well. These are good places for dairy farms because cows eat a lot of grass.

Cows on dairy farms are milked twice a day, seven days a week.

In the milking shed: The cows are milked in milking sheds by milking machines. Most machines have one or two rows of cups, with about ten to twelve cups in each row. Some really big milking sheds can have machines with fifty cups.

Before the cows are milked, their udders are washed. Then the four teat cups, or suckers, are put on each cow's udders. The cow begins to give milk when she feels the milking machine put on her udder. The suckers squeeze the milk from the cow just like a calf does.

Milking: Most cows give ten litres of milk each time they are milked, but this can vary, depending on the health and breed of the cow and how old it is. After a cow has been milked, the farmer usually sprays the cow's udders with antiseptic. This helps to kill germs and keep the cow clean and healthy.

The milk that has been sucked from the cow is pumped along pipes to a vat, which is a huge stainless-steel tank. The milk is kept cool, to 4 degrees Celsius or below, and filtered to make sure it is clean.

farm

Collecting the milk:

Milking sheds must be kept very clean, so all parts of the shed and the equipment are washed after each milking. All parts of the machine, including the pumps, pipes and tanks are steam-cleaned twice a day.

Milk-tankers collect the milk from the farms. These tankers come daily to large farms, and three or four times a week to smaller farms.

Milk-tankers deliver the milk to dairy factories.

Pasteurising the milk:

In the dairy factory, milk is poured into huge stainless-steel vats and pasteurised. Pasteurisation is the heating and cooling process that kills germs in the milk.

Pasteurised milk is then bottled by machines. Milk put into cartons must be homogenised — the process of squirting milk through tiny holes. This breaks up the fat so that it does not rise to the surface.

Milk is either sold for drinking or used by the dairy factory to produce other dairy products, such as butter, cream, cheese, ice-cream and yoghurt.

The City Despatch

Chocolate Bar Arrested!

*from our city reporter
Clifford Jefferson*

The problem of spruikers who annoy business people and shoppers on our town's streets may soon be solved.

Mrs Christine Waters, 39, of Blandest Heights, was arrested yesterday for allegedly spruiking outside the premises of Lower Than the Lowest Discount Goodies while dressed as a two-metre-high chocolate bar.

Waters is the fifth person to be arrested in the last two weeks, as the local council continues its campaign to clamp down on spruiking by enforcing its anti-spruiking laws.

"We're determined to clean up this city," said Mayor Helen Snitch. "Spruiking is noisy, obstructive, unsightly, and people are complaining about it. We are simply responding to public demand."

Mayor Snitch added that she personally had been a victim of spruiking. "I was accosted by a giant banana who told me I needed to eat more fruit and vegetables," she said. "It was very annoying."

Mrs Waters was arrested after she was observed allegedly approaching people and encouraging them to eat more sweets, especially the brand of chocolate sold by her employer.

Reggie Masters, spokesperson for Lower Than the Lowest Discount Goodies, said his company would consult their solicitors regarding a possible lawsuit against the council.

Other spruikers charged in the last two weeks include a man dressed as a giant teddy bear, and two women dressed as a pair of running shoes.

SPRUIKERS OPPRESSED!

by Dorita Sledge

In a fiery speech at last night's council meeting, a spokesperson for the Australian Spruikers Union, Ms Aubrey Giddle, described the council's anti-spruiking law as high-handed, and a devastating blow for small business.

As protesters chanted angrily outside, Ms Giddle demanded that the council's oppressive law be overturned. "In light of yesterday's outrageous arrest of Christine Waters, we have no choice but to file suit," she said. "We'll take this to the highest court if we have to."

A tearful Christine Waters moved the protesters with her story. "I'd been out of work for almost a year when I got that spruiking job," she said. "I was proud to put on that chocolate bar suit because it meant I had the dignity of finally working again."

Reggie Masters, spokesperson for Lower Than the Lowest Discount Goodies, where Ms Waters was employed, berated the council for interfering in his right to engage in commerce. And union member Kev Lissard pointed to spruiking's long and honourable history. "Town criers, that's what we are. Town criers. It's just that today's news and gossip is about how much stuff costs and how you can save money. That's the only difference between me and some old geezer in funny pants from a few hundred years ago."

Mayor Helen Snitch was unavailable for comment.

At the Power Plant

Ms Frizzle and her class are on a school excursion to visit a power plant. But this will be no ordinary school excursion...

Up ahead was the town's power plant. It looked like a little city of buildings.

"Inside those buildings is the equipment that makes electricity, class," Ms Frizzle told us.

"Oooh, let's visit the power plant now," suggested Ms Frizzle's niece.

"What a wonderful idea, Dottie!" crowed the Friz. "Hang on, everyone!"

When we arrived at the plant, Ms Frizzle gave us heat-proof suits and said, "We'll begin our tour by observing the fuel supply."

She pushed a little button on the dashboard, and the bus changed into a dump truck. "Making a delivery!" Ms Frizzle yelled.

The dump truck tipped up, and we went tumbling down the coal chute. We landed in the coal bin and slid right into a furnace of flames.

"Let's see what all this heat is used for," said Ms Frizzle.

Overhead, there was a metal pipe with water in it. The fire was making the water boil. And the boiling water was turning into steam.

"Hold hands, everyone!" yelled the Friz. She jumped up to the pipe, pulling us along.

In a second, our whole class was inside the steam pipe. The steam was travelling at high speed—and we were, too.

"Now we'll learn what all this steam is used for, class," called Ms Frizzle. We steamed along through the pipe and into the next room in the power plant.

There was only one thing in the room—an enormous machine called a turbine. It had blades like a fan, and when the steam pushed on the blades, the turbine spun around.

The turbine made a metal shaft spin, too. We spun around the shaft and slid along to the next part of the power plant.

"Let's go look at what all this spinning is used for," said the Friz cheerfully.

We were too dizzy to reply.

The shaft led us to the generator—the part of the plant that actually makes electricity.

This generator was *really* big, but it worked just like the little one we had made in school!

On the outside were coils of wire. On the inside was a magnet. The shaft turned the magnet, and the moving magnet made electric current run in the wire.

Then the current flowed into a power line; a large wire that was leading out of the plant.

"Next we'll observe what all this electricity is used for," said the Friz.

Suddenly we began to get smaller...and smaller...and smaller...until we could fit inside the power line.

We got even smaller.

Now we could fit between the spaces in the wire. Electrons were jumping all around us, making the current.

The coal fire made the steam...   that turned the turbine...   that turned the shaft...   that turned the magnet...

We followed the Friz from the power plant through the lines towards our town, dodging electrons as we went.

On the way, we passed through transformers, devices that made the voltage in the wire higher or lower.

Higher voltage helps the current travel the long distance from the plant to the places that will use the electricity. Lower voltages are used in factories and big businesses. Still lower voltages are used in small buildings and homes.

"Where are we going?" someone asked.

"We're on our way to a light bulb," the Friz answered calmly.

We were moving down the power line when Ms Frizzle said, "Here we are at the town library."

We followed her through the wires and into a lamp.

"We're going right into the light bulb!" Wanda cried.

Inside the bulb, we squeezed into a very, very, very thin wire—the filament.

"The filament makes the bulb light up," said Ms Frizzle.

Billions and billions of electrons were pushing through the thin filament all at once. That made the filament get white-hot. When something is white-hot, it glows with light.

We scarcely had time to put on our sunglasses before we were in and out of the bulb. Then we were heading away from the library. We didn't even have a chance to check out any books!

We travelled down the street through the power line until we came to Jo's Diner.

that made electricity.

Transformer

I hope Phoebe likes this

Once inside the restaurant, we entered a toaster. "Now we'll observe how electricity makes heat," said the Friz. "Follow me into the heating element!"

The heating element was a coil made of a special kind of wire. When electricity flowed through the wire, it got red-hot!

The heating element was making some toast.

That reminded us—wasn't it almost lunchtime?

Ms Frizzle didn't stop. Maybe she wasn't hungry.

She went out the wire into the main power line again. "We will now visit someone's house," she said, making a sharp turn.

"I wonder whose house," murmured Phoebe.

It was Phoebe's house! Her grandma was using a power saw to make a bookcase for Phoebe's room.

"Oh good," said Ms Frizzle. "This gives us a chance to see how the saw is driven by an electric motor."

Ms Frizzle said an electric motor has magnets inside. "Remember how we made electric current with a magnet?" asked Frizzie. "Well, it works the other way, too. Electric current can turn a piece of metal into a magnet. This kind of magnet is called an electromagnet. Electromagnets are what make the motor run."

"Now for a tour of the electric motor," called Ms Frizzle.

from *The Magic School Bus and the Electric Field Trip* by Joanna Cole

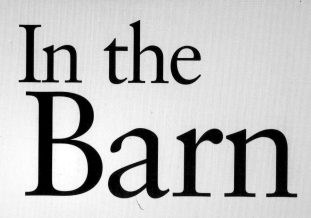

In the Barn

The barn was the most important place on Zuckerman's farm. Here the dramas of the lives of the animals, Charlotte the spider and Wilbur the pig, were played out as the children played.

Day after day the spider waited, head-down, for an idea to come to her. Hour by hour she sat motionless, deep in thought. Having promised Wilbur that she would save his life, she was determined to keep her promise.

Charlotte was naturally patient. She knew from experience that if she waited long enough, a fly would come to her web; and she felt sure that if she thought long enough about Wilbur's problem, an idea would come to her mind.

Finally, one morning towards the middle of July, the idea came. "Why, how perfectly simple!" she said to herself. "The way to save Wilbur's life is to play a trick on Zuckerman."

If I can fool a bug, thought Charlotte, I can surely fool a man. People are not as smart as bugs.

Wilbur walked into his yard just at that moment. "What are you thinking about, Charlotte?" he asked.

"I was just thinking," said the spider, "that people are very gullible."

"What does 'gullible' mean?"

"Easy to fool," said Charlotte.

"That's a mercy," replied Wilbur, and he lay down in the shade of his fence and went fast asleep. The spider, however, stayed wide awake, gazing affectionately at him and making plans for his future.

Summer was half gone. She knew she didn't have much time.

That morning, just as Wilbur fell asleep, Avery Arable wandered into the Zuckermans' front yard, followed by Fern. Avery carried a live frog in his hand. Fern had a crown of daisies in her hair. The children ran for the kitchen.

"Just in time for a piece of blueberry pie," said Mrs Zuckerman.

"Look at my frog!" said Avery, placing the frog on the drainboard and holding out his hand for pie.

"Take that thing out of here!" said Mrs Zuckerman.

"He's hot," said Fern. "He's almost dead, that frog."

"He is not," said Avery. "He lets me scratch him between the eyes." The frog jumped and landed in Mrs Zuckerman's dishpan full of soapy water.

"You're getting your pie on you," said Fern. "Can I look for eggs in the henhouse, Aunt Edith?"

"Run outdoors, both of you! And don't bother the hens!"

"It's getting all over everything," shouted Fern. "His pie is all over his front."

"Come on, frog!" cried Avery. He scooped up his frog. The frog kicked, splashing soapy water on to the blueberry pie.

"Another crisis!" groaned Fern.

"Let's swing in the swing!" said Avery.

The children ran to the barn. Mr Zuckerman had the best swing in the country. It was a single long piece of heavy rope tied to the beam over the north doorway.

At the bottom end of the rope was a fat knot to sit on. It was arranged so that you could swing without being pushed. You climbed a ladder to the hayloft. Then, holding the rope, you stood at the edge and looked down, and were scared and dizzy. Then you straddled the knot, so that it acted as a seat. Then you got up all your nerve, took a deep breath, and jumped. For a second you seemed to be falling to the barn floor far below, but then suddenly the rope would begin to catch you, and you would sail through the barn door going a mile a minute, with the wind whistling in your eyes and ears and hair.

Then you would zoom upwards into the sky, and look up at the clouds, and the rope would twist and you would twist and turn with the rope. Then you would drop down, down, down out of the sky and come sailing back into the barn almost into the hayloft, then sail out again (not quite so far this time), then in again (not quite so high), then out again, then in again, then out, then in; and then you'd jump off and fall down and let somebody else try it.

Mothers for miles around worried about Zuckerman's swing. They feared some child would fall off. But no child ever did. Children almost always hang on to things tighter than their parents think they will.

Avery put the frog in his pocket and climbed to the hayloft. "The last time I swang in this swing, I almost crashed into a barn swallow," he yelled.

"Take that frog out!" ordered Fern.

Avery straddled the rope and jumped. He sailed out through the door, frog and all, and into the sky, frog and all. Then he sailed back into the barn.

"Your tongue is purple!" screamed Fern.

"So is yours!" cried Avery, sailing out again with the frog.

"I have hay inside my dress! It itches!" called Fern.

"Scratch it!" yelled Avery, as he sailed back.

"It's my turn," said Fern. "Jump off!"

"Fern's got the itch!" sang Avery.

When he jumped off, he threw the swing up to his sister. She shut her eyes tight and jumped. She felt the dizzy drop, then the supporting lift of the swing.

When she opened her eyes she was looking up into the blue sky and was about to fly back through the door.

They took turns for an hour.

from *Charlotte's Web* by E. B. White

FARMYARD

The Purple Cow
I never saw a Purple Cow,
I never hope to see one;
But I can tell you anyhow,
I'd rather see than be one.

Gelett Burgess

The Cow
The cow is of bovine ilk;
One end is moo, the other, milk.

Ogden Nash

Why Do Sheep
Why do sheep
have curly coats?

To keep the wind
out of their froats.

Roger McGough

FUNNIES

What do you get if you lie under a cow?
A pat on the head.

Where does a cow like to go on Saturday afternoons?
To the moo-vies.

What side of a cow do you milk it on?
The udder side.

Why do cows wear bells around their necks?
Because their horns don't work.

What do you get if you cross a chicken with a cow?
Roost beef.

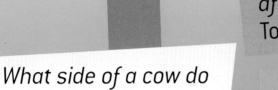

What do you get when you cross a kangaroo and a sheep? A woolly jumper.

What happened when the chook swallowed a yo-yo?
She laid the same egg three times.

What do you get when you cross a chook and a dog?
Pooched eggs.

What do you get when you cross a chook with a bell?
An alarm cluck.

Ring

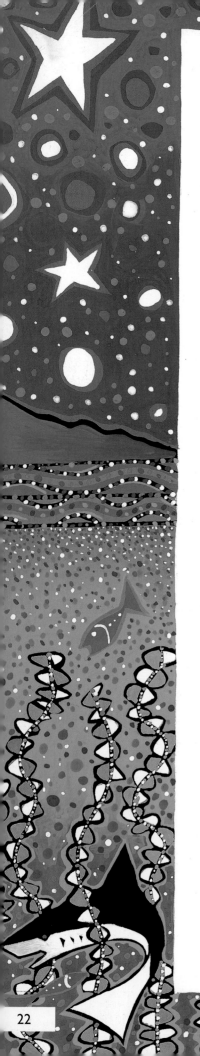

BARACUMA'S FISHING NET

Melva Jean Roberts

Baracuma owned the only fishing net in the world. It was so good that when he cast it into the water, the net immediately filled with fish. Wandi, a friend from a neighbouring tribe, heard the story of the wonderful net and begged Baracuma to allow him to use it.

Baracuma refused to lend the net, because he knew that if it was out of his possession for any length of time he would die. Wandi pleaded with Baracuma, assuring him that he would return the net promptly. Baracuma, persuaded against his better judgment, allowed Wandi to take the net away.

However, the fish were so plentiful that Wandi forgot his promise until darkness forced him to return the net. To his dismay, he found that Baracuma was dead. He tried all night to bring his friend back to life, but without success.

Wandi was so ashamed over the result of his selfishness that he changed himself into a hawk and flew to the top of a high tree.

An old Kangaroo-man heard that Baracuma had died for his generosity, and used magical powers to restore him to life in the form of a native cat.

The Aborigines believed that this is why Wandi the hawk lives and nests high in the treetops, and hunts for his food during the day, while Baracuma the native cat avoids the selfish Wandi by making his home underground and catching lizards and other small creatures during the hours of darkness.

Koolulla and the Two Sisters

Melva Jean Roberts

Two sisters lived deep in the ocean in a vast forest of kelp. Sometimes, they came up on the shore to search for crabs and shellfish among the rocks, and on one of these occasions, they were so busy at their task that they did not see that Koolulla, who was a renowned hunter, was camped nearby.

Koolulla had been casting his net in the shallows, and had just finished cooking his catch when he saw the sisters. He was so impressed by their beauty that he resolved to capture them, and so he picked up his net and a large firestick from the fire and crept close enough to the two women to throw his net over them.

One wriggled out from under it and jumped back into the sea.

Quickly, Koolulla secured the net around his one captive and leaped into the water, chasing after the other sister. As his firestick sank, it created a burst of sparks which floated up into the sky.

Koolulla swam all that day in pursuit of the woman, but she finally led him into the kelp forest. There, exhausted and entangled in the great mass of seaweed, he sank to the bottom and was transformed into the shark, compelled always to hunt the deep waters in search of the woman he lost.

The sister on the shore, unable to free herself from Koolulla's net, eventually died and was changed into the evening star. The sparks from Koolulla's firestick may still be seen in the sky. They are the first stars to appear as night falls, and the brightest of them all is the evening star, keeping watch over her sister who still lives in the underwater forest.

The Fish with the Deep Sea Smile

They fished and they fished
Way down in the sea
Down in the sea a mile
They fished among all the fish in the sea
For the fish with the deep sea smile.

One fish came up from the deep of the sea
From down in the sea a mile
It had blue eyes
And whiskers three
But never a deep sea smile.

One fish came up from the deep of the sea
From down in the sea a mile
With electric lights up and down his tail
But never a deep sea smile.

They fished and they fished
Way down in the sea
Down in the sea a mile
They fished among all the fish in the sea
For the fish with a deep sea smile.

One fish came up with terrible teeth
One fish with long strong jaws
One fish came up with long stalked eyes
One fish with terrible claws.

They fished all through the ocean deep
For many and many a mile
And they caught a fish with a laughing eye
But none with a deep sea smile.

And then one day they got a pull
From down in the sea a mile
And when they pulled the fish into the boat
HE SMILED A DEEP SEA SMILE.

And as he smiled, the hook got free
And then, what a deep sea smile!
He flipped his tail and swam away
Down in the sea a mile.

Margaret Wise Brown

Helpful Harry

READERS' THEATRE

Cast: <u>Narrator, Harry, Angus, Abbie, Lochie, Harry's dad</u>

ALL: Helpful Harry written by Kerri Lane

Narrator: Helpful Harry had an idea how he could help his father win the animal parade at the local fair. Harry decided that by using his chemistry set, he could add a bit of colour to the animals so that they looked their best.

Abbie, Lochie, Angus: What are you doing?

Harry: Oh! It's only you lot. You scared the life out of me.

Abbie: Why are you scared? What are you doing?

Harry: Nothing.

Abbie: Yes you are!

Harry: It's nothing. I...it's a secret.

Lochie: What kind of secret?

Abbie: Why are your chooks drinking this blue stuff?

Harry: Blue? Oh no! Not *blue!*

Angus: I drink blue drinks sometimes. Blue is okay...

Harry: Not this time. Blue is bad! *Very bad!* Quick chookies—shoo! Shoo!

Narrator: Lochie, Abbie, Angus and Harry began chasing the chooks away from the blue drink, but it was no use. The chooks kept darting between their legs to get back to the blue drink.

Angus: Quick, Lochie! Take that stuff outside!

Narrator:	As soon as Lochie disappeared out of the shed, the chooks became quieter. But Harry didn't. Because before his very eyes, his father's prize chooks were starting to turn...
All:	*Blue!*
Harry:	I wanted to help Dad. They were supposed to turn red. I read this old science recipe. It said if you mixed this stuff properly and drink lots of it, you'd turn that colour. I mixed up a few colours until I got the red right. But, I must have knocked over the blue dye when you came in.
Angus, Lochie:	Oh, sorry.
Abbie:	Does this drink hurt the chooks?
Harry:	No, it wears off in a couple of weeks.
Abbie:	So, what's your problem?
Harry:	My problem is that the fair is tomorrow. Dad is going to be really mad with me.
Abbie:	Why can't we just give them some red drink now?
Harry:	Do you think it would work?
Angus, Lochie:	Don't know.
Narrator:	It took no time to fill up the buckets with the special red drink.
Harry:	It's working! They're changing to... to...
All:	*Purple!*
Harry:	Oh, no! Dad's best chooks are purple!
Abbie:	Oops! I forgot blue and red make purple.
Narrator:	Harry snatched up the bottles of dye he'd made. There was only yellow left.
Harry:	Get these bottles out of here!
Lochie:	I'll put them in those buckets.

Helpful Harry (continued)

Angus:	Just take them as far away from this chook shed as you can!
Abbie:	At least your dad has still got Blossom, the jersey cow, and Simon the goat. Maybe they'll win...
Lochie:	We might have another problem.
Harry:	I don't think I want to know about it.
Lochie:	When I went out to get the buckets of blue drink—one was empty.
Harry, Abbie, Angus:	What?
Abbie:	I hope your dad isn't too upset about only entering Blossom, because I don't think a *blue* Angora goat is going to win.
Harry:	Oh, no. Not Simon, too.
Angus:	Lochie, I hope you got rid of that other bucket.
Lochie:	Yep. I put it at the edge of that empty paddock.
Harry:	Blossom's paddock?
Lochie:	Yeah, but she wasn't there.
Harry:	Are you sure? Sometimes she hides behind that big tree...

[*The four friends stop and look at each other.*]

All:	Quick, run!
Lochie:	I'm sure it's okay. I tipped the yellow into the blue and that made...
All:	*Green!*

Narrator:	There was Blossom as bright and happy as could be—and very, very green.
Harry:	I am in deep trouble, now.
Abbie:	Actually, there might be a way out of this. We could paint them back to their original colours.
Harry:	You think we should *paint* all the animals back to their right colours?
Abbie:	We could use water-based paints. They won't hurt the animals. They'll just wash off. Like face paints—kind of ...
Lochie:	Where would we get enough water-based paints to do a whole cow? We'd need heaps of it.
Abbie:	My sister's an art teacher. She's got huge buckets of this powder stuff at home.
Narrator:	It took only a few minutes to come to a decision. Abbie was soon back with the paint.
Abbie:	I can still just make out Blossom's markings. It'll be like using a stencil.
Narrator:	Abbie and Angus struggled into the paddock carrying the brown and white paint. They grabbed big brushes and started to paint. The black and white goat didn't prove to be too much of a problem for Lochie. But the chooks were a different matter. Harry had to spray paint them! It was hard work, but soon it was all done. Now they just had to keep all the animals away from Harry's dad—and any water. They'd just closed the shed door when Harry's dad rumbled along on his old tractor.
Harry's dad:	Hi kids! Ready for the fair tomorrow?
Harry:	As ready as we'll ever be.

Pot Luck

Chris McTrustry

Cedric 'Scoop' Tellall, ace reporter, pushed his way to the front of the crowd. Big crowds always meant a story, and he wanted to find out what this one was all about.

His daughter, Hannah, followed along behind.

Scoop gasped when he saw an elderly lady dressed in mud-spattered overalls standing in the middle of a field, in front of a bulldozer.

"Who is that silly person?" he asked loudly.

A boy standing beside Scoop glared up at him. "That's my grandma," said the boy, Josh. "And she's not silly. She's protesting."

"Oh, sorry," said Scoop.

"I'll ask the next question, Dad," said Hannah. She smiled at the boy and asked, "Why is your grandma covered in little dots of mud?"

"That's my fault," answered Josh. "I was playing with Grandma's potter's wheel and accidentally sprayed mud on her. You see, I didn't know I had to—"

But the bulldozer rumbling into life cut short Josh's explanation.

"I'm going to demolish that cottage right now!" the driver bellowed.

Josh couldn't believe his eyes—the bulldozer was going to run over Grandma!

"Get out of the way, Gran!" he yelled.

The bulldozer rumbled forward. But Grandma planted her hands on her hips and stuck out her chin defiantly.

"Never!" she yelled.

The driver stopped the bulldozer and climbed down.

The crowd of onlookers cheered.

"I'm going to call my boss," the driver yelled. "He's going to be very angry!"

Grandma turned and waved to the onlookers.

"Friends, neighbours, thank you for your support," she said. "I shall stop these road-builders destroying my cottage."

Again, the onlookers cheered.

"You're the coolest, Grandma," said Josh.

"Yeah," said Hannah. "Cool, calm and collected."

Grandma smiled and wrapped an arm around Josh. "Come along," she said. "Let's go inside for refreshments!" She smiled and nodded at Hannah. "You can bring your new friend if you like."

Soon, Grandma, Josh, Hannah and Scoop were settled around Grandma's huge kitchen table. "I don't normally talk to the press, Mr Tellall," said Grandma, pouring cups of tea for the adults and lemonade for the children.

"Dad isn't a normal reporter," said Hannah. "He finds out about people in trouble and tells the whole world about them. Maybe he can help you save your cottage."

"Wow," said Josh. "Could you, Mr Tellall?"

"I can usually sniff out a good story," said Scoop, tilting back his head and sniffing long and loud. "And I can smell one… right here."

"Why don't you take these guys to court and get a judge to stop them?" asked Hannah.

"That's a good idea, Hannah," said Grandma. "But lawyers cost more money than I have."

"Then we'll just have to raise it," said Josh with great determination.

Scoop sniffed again. "I definitely smell a story," he said.

Grandma decided to have a Save-The-Cottage garage sale and Josh and Hannah offered to help search the cottage to find things to sell.

"Let's search the garden shed, too," said Josh. "It's full of old junk."

He pointed across the yard to a large, muddied potter's wheel that was sitting under an apple tree. "I found that in the shed," he said.

"It looks really old," said Hannah.

"It is," said Josh. "And it's loads of fun."

Not having any time to waste, Grandma arranged for the garage sale to be the next weekend. Everyone in the village came to see what was on offer.

"That pottery on the end table," Scoop said to Grandma. "It looks very valuable."

"It is," said Grandma. "Those pieces were made by a famous potter who they say lived in this very village."

Scoop sniffed and whipped out his note pad. "And his name?" he said.

"Not him," said Grandma with a smile. "Her. Alice Ponsby."

"I've heard of her!" Scoop exclaimed. "She's famous. You can't sell that!"

That evening, Grandma, Josh, Hannah and Scoop counted the money they'd made.

"I don't think this is nearly enough for a lawyer," said Grandma. "I do wish you hadn't talked me out of selling my Ponsby pottery."

The following day, a man called by and told Grandma the court had ordered her to move out of the cottage.

The day after that, Grandma's belongings were moved out.

And the day after that was the day chosen to demolish Grandma's cottage.

A storm raged in Josh's stomach as he watched the workers pick up their sledgehammers and stomp into Grandma's cottage. And when he heard the first sledgehammer slam into a wall inside the cottage, he couldn't bear it. He scrambled under the safety barriers and raced inside.

A workman was standing in the sitting room, his sledgehammer raised, just about to smash another hole in the wall.

"Stop!" yelled Josh. "You can't do this!"

The surprised workman dropped his sledgehammer and, mumbling to himself, hurried off to find his boss.

Soon after, the boss stormed into the sitting room. Grandma, Hannah and Scoop followed close behind.

"Do you want to get yourself hurt, son?" said the angry boss. "It's dangerous in here!"

Josh pointed to the large hole in the wall. "Look what they've done to your cottage, Grandma."

"I know, Josh," said Grandma sadly. "But there's nothing we can do about it."

Hannah peered into the hole. "Hey!" she gasped. "There's something in there!"

"It's a painting," said the boss, as he carefully lifted it out. It was a picture of Grandma's cottage.

"Good grief!" said Scoop. "The date on this painting is 1841!"

"But the cottage looks just like it does today," said Hannah.

"And look here," said Josh, pointing at the painting. "There's a lady using a pottery wheel in the front garden!"

Hannah peered closely at the lady and the pottery wheel. "It looks exactly like the old one under the apple tree," she said.

"It probably is," said Grandma. "That pottery wheel is very old."

"There's a name," said Hannah excitedly. "In the bottom right-hand corner." She squinted at the faded signature. "Albert Ponsby."

Everyone gasped in surprise.

"Then that would mean the woman in the painting is Albert's wife—Alice Ponsby, the famous potter," said Scoop.

"And that means you have her potter's wheel, Grandma," said Josh.

"It must be worth a fortune," said Hannah.

Scoop looked at Grandma with wide, happy eyes. "So," he said, "you have Alice Ponsby's potter's wheel. And this painting proves the Ponsbys lived right here. That means no-one will be allowed to pick a flower from the garden, much less knock down the cottage."

"Really?" said Josh and Hannah.

"Most certainly," said Scoop. "This cottage is an historical site. It must be preserved."

"Talk about pot luck," muttered the boss.

Then Grandma did something she hadn't done in many days—she smiled.

"I think your story will have a very happy ending, Scoop," she said.

THE END

Why Can't You Get a Proper Job?

Shelley's mum, Anne, has a new job. But Shelley is less than impressed, especially as she has to stay with Mrs Murray …

At first, Anne tried coaxing. "You'd really like it, Shelley," she said. "They have table tennis and a craft room and a lovely indoor pool."

But Shelley translated the coaxing into brain-washing. "I'm not coming," she said angrily. "I already told you a million times that I want to stay home by myself! I don't see why I'm not allowed. Petra Van Rees stays home by herself two whole nights a week when her mum goes to aerobics."

"I don't care what Petra does." Her mother's voice shed some of its patience. "You're not old enough to be left alone in the evenings, even if it is only till quarter to ten. That house round the corner got broken into last month…"

"As if anyone would want to bust into our house! As if there's anything here worth pinching!" Shelley regretted saying that, for her mother's face looked suddenly hurt and vulnerable, but the regret didn't last for more than a few seconds. She was too angry. "Having to go next door to stay with that boring old Mrs Murray every single night for the rest of the holidays!"

"You know I'll be having Sunday evenings off."

"Big deal! Megan Webb is going away to the Gold Coast. We never go anywhere posh like that! I don't know why you can't get a proper job, anyhow. Petra's mum has a great one managing a music shop and Petra gets cassettes half-price any time she wants, and she's going away for the holidays, too. Anyway, even if she

wasn't, I bet she wouldn't have to go next door and stay with a boring old lady when she could be home in her own place watching TV!"

"I've already said that you can come with me to the nursing home and use the pool there. You don't *have* to go to Mrs Murray's every night. And, Shelley, you should realise that I was lucky to get this job. Any job. I'm not really qualified for anything in particular. Anyhow, I can't stay here arguing; I've got to leave in five minutes. If you're sure you won't change your mind and come with me, then run along over to Mrs Murray's. And for goodness' sake, stop that silly sulking."

Shelley stormed next door with a face as fierce as a hawk and rang Mrs Murray's doorbell, determined to find no pleasure in the three hours' enforced stay.

Mrs Murray was a cheerful, kind, aunty sort of person. As soon as Shelley was sitting down she got out the album of her son's recent wedding. Shelley glanced

through it, making hardly any effort to disguise her
boredom.

When Mrs Murray made tea and produced a plate
of delectable sponge fingers, Shelley took only one and
said that she wasn't hungry. She kept her nose in a
library book, even though it was dull, and resisted Mrs
Murray's attempts at conversation.

"Some kind of nursing home, is it, where your mum's
working now?" Mrs Murray asked, comfortably knitting
away at a baby's jacket for her daughter's expected baby.
"I think your mum's wonderful to take on a job like that."

"It's sort of a hostel. I don't know much about it. You'll have to ask her when she gets home," Shelley said curtly, pretending that she'd reached an exciting part of the book and didn't want to be interrupted. She felt ashamed that Anne was working in such a place. None of the other kids at school had mothers working in a job like that.

"A hostel for mentally and physically handicapped people," Mrs Murray said, maddeningly chatty.

Shelley didn't answer and flipped over an unread page. She should be able to see that I'm too annoyed to chat, too annoyed to do anything except huddle in the middle of my rage, she thought.

"She'll be tired when she gets home. She's lucky she's got you, Shelley, to help her with the housework and that."

Mrs Murray switched on the TV for the eight-thirty film.

Shelley watched impatiently for ten minutes and decided that the film was the sloppiest she'd ever seen. "Can I use your phone, please?' she asked, heading towards the hallway and the phone table before Mrs Murray had even nodded.

She phoned Petra, who was starry with excitement because she was going away for a holiday at a children's country guest house.

Shelley tried to sound interested, but felt overwhelmed by jealousy and self-pity. It wasn't fair! Her mother hadn't been able to afford a holiday, and now she would be on duty at that wretched hostel for four weeks, too. Four weeks of spending every evening with Mrs Murray! It just wasn't fair!

from Boss of the Pool by Robin Klein

Joel's Diary

Julie Mitchell

Monday 14 March

Dear Diary,
Ever since Grandpa died, Grandma's been talking about the mountains where she was born. Her stories make me wish that I could live in the mountains too— and GUESS WHAT! We're going to move there! Our house here in Mayville is already up for sale.

I can't wait for my first winter in the mountains. The snow will be fantastic! Grandma says there's so much of it that I can make whole families of snowpeople if I want to.

Joel

Thursday 17 March

Dear Diary,
As soon as I get home from school each day, I ask Grandma if anyone bought the house. But the answer's always no. Grandma keeps telling me not to give up hope, but I'm starting to think we'll be stuck in Mayville forever.

Joel

Friday 31 March

Dear Diary,
It took ages, but someone finally bought the house! Grandma and I are driving to the mountains to look for a new house on the weekend. I can't wait!

Joel

Friday 12 May

Dear Diary,
Sorry I haven't written for a long time, but so much has happened. First, Grandma and I found a house we liked on Mount Tibbet. Then we had to pack our things for the move. The new house is smaller than our old one, so we had a garage sale to get rid of the stuff we didn't need. (I kept all my books. Grandma says they'll keep me entertained when it's too cold to play outside.)

We moved to the new house three days ago. And since then we've been busy unpacking and exploring.

Tomorrow morning we're going to see how far up the mountain we can climb.

Joel

Tuesday 16 May

Dear Diary,
I saw that lizard again today, and you'll never guess what happened—IT SPOKE TO ME!! (Not out loud—kind of inside my head.)

I told Grandma about it, but she's having a hard time believing me—and an even harder time believing what the lizard said.

It said it's not a lizard at all—it's a dragon. And it needs a safe place to live until it grows up. I'm so happy because it asked if it could stay with us and Grandma said yes.

I wonder how long it takes for a dragon to grow up?

Joel

Sunday 14 May

Dear Diary,
Grandma and I made it all the way to the top of Mount Tibbet! I was really tired when we got back, so I decided to go to bed early.

A strange sound kept me awake, though. It was coming from the knapsack we'd taken on our climb. I was terrified a snake had wriggled in there, but it turned out to be a lizard.

I don't think it's a normal lizard, though. When I told it to go outside, it looked up at me and I got the feeling it could understand what I was saying.

Joel

A Timeline of the Disc

600 BC: Thales of Miletus (Greece) observed that after he rubbed a piece of amber with a cloth, the amber attracted bits of feather and plant material. Our word for electricity comes from the Greek word for amber "elektron".

1646: Sir Thomas Browne (England) used the word "electricity" for the first time.

1700: Stephen Gray discovered that some substances conduct electricity and some do not.

1733: Charles Dufey (France) experimented with the conduction of electricity.

1746-1752: Benjamin Franklin (USA) developed the theory that electricity consisted of a single fluid. He was the first person to use the terms "positive" and "negative". Franklin performed an experiment, flying a kite in a storm. He showed that lightning is electricity.

1785: Charles Coulomb (France) worked out the laws of attraction and repulsion between electrically charged bodies.

1800: Alessandro Volta (Italy) built the first battery.

1820: Hans Christian Oersted (Denmark) discovered electromagnetism. He discovered that a current flowing through a wire would move a compass needle. This showed that an electric current has a magnetic effect.

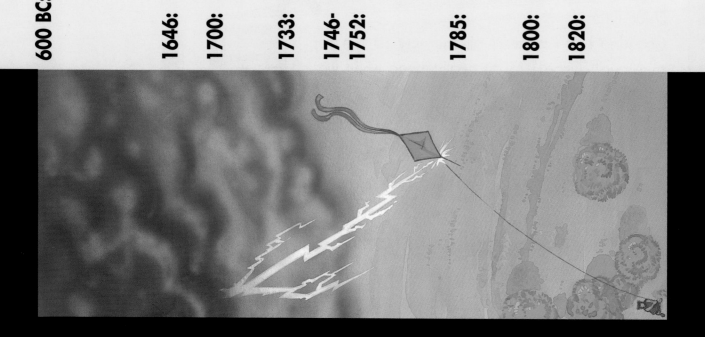

44

...overy of Electricity

1820s: Andre-Marie Ampere (France) measured the magnetic effect of an electric current. He worked out the laws that form the basis of the science of current electricity.

1826: Thomas Seebeck (Germany) discovered that heat can produce electricity.

1831: Michael Faraday (England) and Joseph Henry (USA) separately found that a moving magnet would cause an electric current in a coil of wire. Even today, all generators and transformers work on the scientific principles discovered by Faraday and Henry.

1880s: Heinrich Hertz (Germany) produced radio waves.

1897: Joseph Thomson discovered that all atoms contain particles of electricity. We now call these particles "electrons". Thomson's discoveries made the electronic age in which we live possible.

1900: John Fleming (Britain) built a vacuum tube that could detect radio signals.

1907: Lee de Forest (USA) invented the tubes that made radio possible.

1920s: The development of vacuum tubes led to the invention of television.

1930s: Radar was invented.

1940s: The first electrical computers were made.

1950s: American and British scientists discovered how to generate electricity using atomic energy.

How I Began My Life in the Workforce

When you turn fifteen, you are old enough to join the workforce.

To get a part-time job, you may have to fill in an application form and go to a job interview. If the employer decides that you are the right person for the organisation, then the process of training and development begins, and you get to join the thousands of people who hold a steady, part-time or casual position, commonly known as a "job".

I started looking for work just before summer. It was the perfect time to look for work because many companies and businesses were looking for extra staff to cope with the holiday rush. Plus it gave me something to do over the summer holidays.

First, I asked my older brothers and sisters how they had found work and if they could give me some advice.

They suggested I try one of the food stores in the large shopping centre near where we live. So I did. I went for a walk to the shops and asked the store manager if there were any vacancies for part-time work and if I could have an application form.

I took the application form home and filled it in.

Then I checked that all the details were correct and I also asked my parents to read over it for me. The next day, I took the form back to the store manager.

A week later, the store manager called and asked me to come in for an interview.

During the interview, I enjoyed a pleasant talk with the store manager and the store's crew trainer. Three days later, the store manager called again. He offered me a part-time job. If I wanted the job, the training would begin in two weeks.

The training involved watching videos about the company and practising the correct procedures at the grill and preparation bench. After a few weeks of this, I was placed on the time sheets and given two 3-hour shifts for the next month.

During the first year of this job, I learnt and gained experience on all different work stations. I became confident and skilled in the grill area, preparing food and serving customers. At the end of the year, I was offered the position of senior crew member.

The part-time job was terrific. It taught me all about teamwork, responsibility, and leadership. It was also great to earn my own money.

I really enjoyed my time in part-time employment and I'm grateful for all the skills I developed during those years. I still use them in my full-time work today.

Energy Moves

Rob Morrison

The sun's heat energy moves to become the energy of the Earth's winds.

Energy from your breakfast moves to your muscles. It becomes mechanical energy when you walk and run.

Energy moves from a swinging pendulum to a clock's mechanism. You can make energy move from one pendulum to another.

You will need:

- 1 piece of string 3 metres long
- 2 pieces of string half a metre long
- two chairs of the same height
- weights (big washers, nuts or lumps of modelling clay)

What to do:

  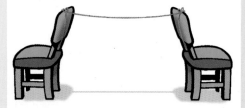 

1 Place the chairs 2 metres apart back-to-back.

2 Tie the long piece of string to the back of the chair so that it hangs between the chairs. The string should be level, but not too tight. It should dip slightly in the middle.

3 Tie the short pieces of string side by side about half a metre apart in the middle of the long string. Tie a weight at the end of each of the short pieces of string to make two pendulums. The weights should be the same size.

What do you see?

The right pendulum begins to swing.

As it does, the left pendulum slows down. Soon the right pendulum is swinging, but the left pendulum has stopped altogether. Then the left pendulum starts to swing again while the right pendulum slows to a stop.

What is happening?

The energy of the swinging pendulum moves into the string and then into the other pendulum.

When all of the energy has moved, the first pendulum is still. Then the energy moves back again. It will keep moving until the energy has gone.

Where does the energy go?

Energy is never lost completely. Energy moves or becomes other forms of energy.

The fibres in the string rub together. Some of the energy is used for that.

Each pendulum makes a tiny wind as it swings. Some energy is used for that.

The tiny wind makes a tiny sound. That is energy, too.

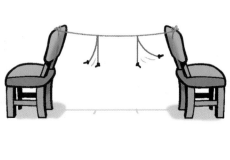

4 Keep the right pendulum still while you pull the left pendulum out sideways. Let the left pendulum go so that it starts swinging.

Make an Origami Frog

You will need a piece of green or brown paper about 14 centimetres square.

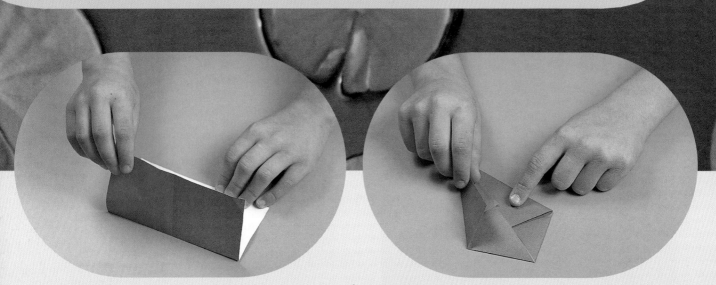

1 Fold the paper in half to make a crease. Open it up again and fold the paper in half the other way.

3 Turn the paper so that it looks like a diamond shape. Fold the top diagonal edges to the centre line to make a kite shape.

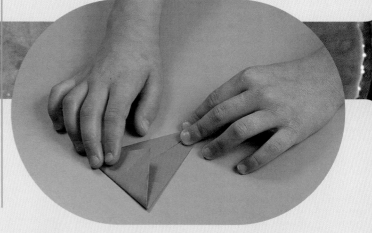

2 Open the paper up and lay it in front of you. Fold the corners to the centre.

4 With the sharp point at the top, fold up the bottom triangle.

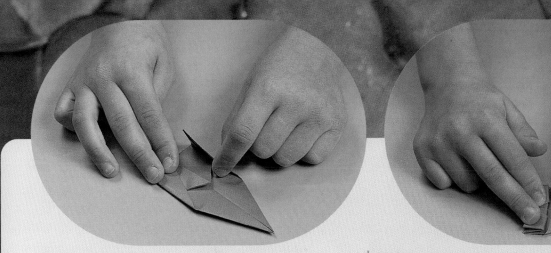

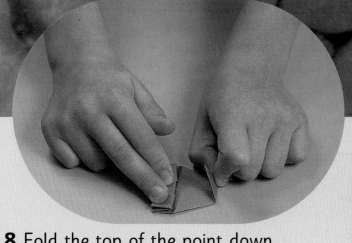

5 Fold both the bottom corners to meet in the centre of the bottom edge.

8 Fold the top of the point down.

6 Hold the paper in your hands with the point to the top and fold the bottom section up.

9 Turn the paper over.

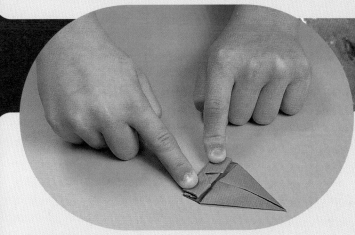

7 Fold the rectangular section back on itself again.

10 Press your finger down on the frog's back. Slide your finger back and let go. Your frog then should jump!

Make a

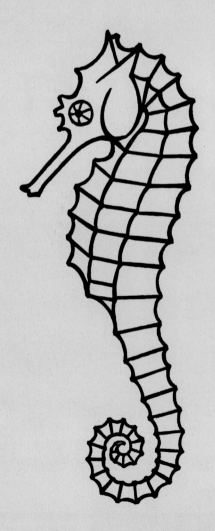

First you need to make your sea horses, then the diorama. To make the sea horses, you will need:

- tracing paper
- thin cardboard
- pens or pencils
- scissors
- sticky tape
- fishing line
- glue

Sea Horse Diorama

Trace the picture of the sea horse. Do this again until you have as many sea horses as you like.

Use scissors to cut out the sea horses.

Paste the sea horse pictures onto cardboard and colour them in.

Stick fishing line to the back of the sea horses. Now, turn over to see how to make the diorama…

A diorama is a model of a scene.

To make the diorama, you will need:

- model sea horses
- a large cardboard box
- glue
- scissors
- paints
- sand
- green and blue cellophane
- green tissue paper
- fishing line
- small rocks
- paintbrush
- sticky tape

5

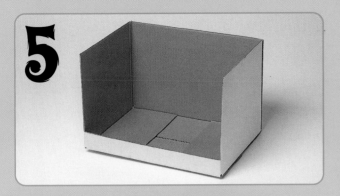

Cut the top and one side off the cardboard box, but leave a small edge at the bottom so the sand won't spill out.

6

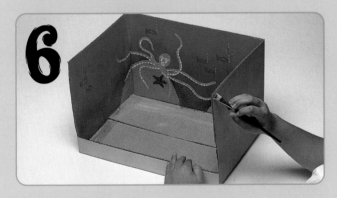

Paint underwater scenes on the inside of the back and sides of the box. Paint the outside of the box.

7

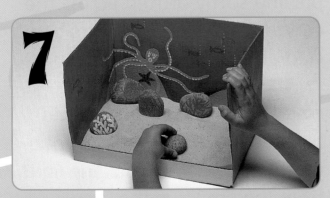

Fill the bottom of the box with sand. Paint some rocks to look like coral and put these in the sand.

8

Make seaweed by twisting tissue paper and cutting strips of green cellophane.

9

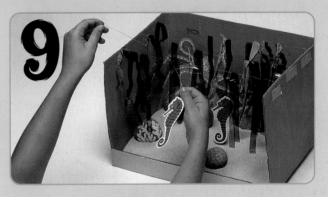

Tape three pieces of fishing line across the top of the diorama. Attach some of the seaweed to the line. Hang the sea horses from the fishing line.

10

Cover the front of the diorama with blue cellophane. Your sea horse diorama is now complete.

Exhausted!

The skiers came in to the campsite slowly—their long trek through the icy mountains was finally over.

They removed their thick gloves and slowly unclipped their skis and boots—those that had enough energy put on warm socks and dry boots. The other skiers just collapsed onto the long verandah of the large timber hut.

The leaders of the camp prepared a huge campfire. The skiers gathered around, and rubbed their hands together and stamped their feet to get the circulation going again. As the skiers became accustomed to the heat of the fire, they slowly relaxed.

They grabbed greedily the jumbo-sized mugs of steaming hot soup offered to them. As they gulped the soup and warmed themselves by the fire, the skiers no longer felt exhausted.

The sun sank slowly in the crystal-blue sky and the skiers looked in wonder at the breathtaking beauty of the soaring mountains.

Soon, the sound of guitars playing softly drifted across the crowd. The skiers began to sing, clap and laugh together.

The flames from the large, crackling campfire danced, and brought a glow to the faces of those gathered around. The light from the fire lit up the snow-sprinkled clearing. The memories of the long and strenuous trek were, for now, forgotten.

Mountain Poems

THE CAMPFIRE

Have you ever seen a campfire?
Log-sparking, flame-leaping, heat-throwing.

THE SNOW TREK

Have you ever been snow trekking?
Toe-numbing, muscle-aching, face-freezing.

THE MOUNTAINS

Have you ever seen the mountains?
Snow-capped, steep-faced, sky-kissing.

The Goat with the Golden Eyes

Nancy Keesing

They are grooming a brindled[1] goat for the judging ring.
His stubbed horns shine with wax, his delicate hooves
Twinkle blacking; his sparse beard combed to a fringe,
Coat crimped and brushed: a most elegant petty King
Whose wives, one lean-ribbed with kid, one heavy with milk,
Nuzzle at hay, awaiting their Lord. They are led
In single file to the grey-dust-coated judge
Who garlands[2] the Attic[3] trio with ribbons of silk;
And the male goat shakes his whiskery head, he sees
An appraising crowd, pricks twitching ears at the noise
Of a bagpipe band.

1 brownish-grey with darker streaks or spots
2 decorates with a wreath of flowers
3 elegant

Descriptive Poem

WATCHING THE JUDGING AT THE FAIR KERRI LANE

It was a very grand fair. There were all sorts of animals. Huge black and white cows and bulls lined up in pens that were full of sweet-smelling, golden straw. One cow let out a huge "moooo" and all the others turned their big, glassy eyes to look at her.

The cows from the O'Neal farm were a bit different. Their coats were so shiny they looked almost like plastic. And they had a funny smell. They didn't smell like the other animals at all.

Beautiful horses with shiny coats were in the next pens along. Their eyes were wide and bright, their ears were pointed and straight and their tails swished quietly from side to side.

There were lots of sheep, too. They looked very fat in their heavy, woollen coats. The wool was grey and fluffy, just like my grandma's tight curls. The sheep were all bleating and I had to cover my ears. It was like being in a room full of people who all had the hiccups!

Then, there were the chooks and roosters. As they walked, their heads jerked from front to back and I found myself doing the same thing. It was catching! Some were snow-white. Others were dark red, with black and orange stripy feathers in their fluffy tails. They clucked and pecked and clucked and pecked.

The goats were next, but just then the trumpet sounded to announce the winners. The trumpeter wasn't very good.

The sound from the trumpet was squawky and screechy. A bit like a parrot with a sore throat.

Owners lined up beside their animals. Some looked nervous as they twisted their fingers together.

Then, everything went quiet as everyone waited for the judges. Even the sheep stopped bleating.

But then the strangest thing happened.

People started screaming and yelling. Horses neighed loudly and stomped their feet. Cows bellowed, chooks clucked and roosters cock-a-doodle-dooed. Of course, the sheep bleated—they never need an excuse.

Everyone looked up to the ceiling. It was raining right through the roof! Soft cold water poured down as if from sprinklers. It *was* from sprinklers!—the special safety sprinklers that turn on in case of fire. Someone had turned them on!

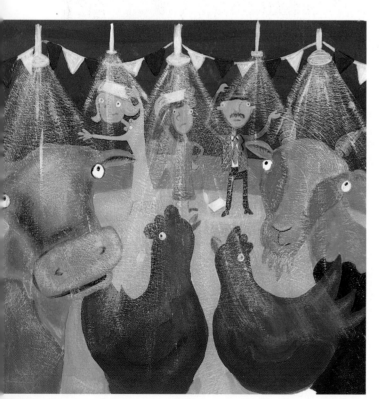

Everyone started to run. Then someone shouted in a strange, loud voice and they all stopped. Soft *oohs* and *ahhs* whispered around the room. Eyes were wide and mouths hung open in amazement.

Some of the animals were changing colour! It was the O'Neal animals. Right before our very eyes, the black and white cows were slowly turning green! As water rushed over the chooks, purple stripes slowly appeared. Then, within moments, they were totally bright purple! They looked just like chewed-up grape bubble-gum! And the goat turned blue! A brilliant blue just like Mum's sapphire ring. It was so pretty!

The funny smell was stronger, too. Then I realised what it was. Paint! That's why the animals had looked like plastic. Someone had painted them.

And I think I know who it was. Over near the door, stood a boy in blue jeans and a paint-splattered t-shirt. He had his face in his hands and he was muttering "I'm really in for it now."

But he didn't get into trouble. In fact, his dad's animals won an award.

The judges gave them a special prize for being presented in such an original manner. The animals accidentally drank food dye! So that explained why they were all such bright colours. The boy, fearing he would get into trouble from his dad, painted over them to make them look normal again.

This was definitely the strangest fair I'd ever been to!

Obentoo

Pamela Rushby

One day, a new kid came to our class. Her name was Yuki. Our teacher asked me to look after her.

Yuki wore a different kind of school uniform to ours—hers looked a bit like a sailor suit. She had trouble understanding us if we spoke quickly. She had a very hi-tech pencil box and backpack. And she was carrying something wrapped in a blue and white scarf and tied with a knot on top.

"What's that?" I asked.

"*Obentoo*," said Yuki.

"What's *obentoo*?" I asked.

Yuki thought for a moment. "Lunch," she said.

Lunch! I'd never seen a lunch wrapped up like that.

At lunchtime, when Yuki untied the scarf, I watched.

"Wow!" I said. I'd never seen a lunch like that before, either. Yuki's obentoo was packed in a pink plastic lunchbox with two chopsticks fitted into a groove on the lid.

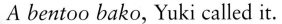

A *bentoo bako*, Yuki called it.

The box had different sections. In the top section was some rice, some *sushi*—rice, prawns and vegetables wrapped in seaweed. And some cucumber.

The bottom section was filled with different things: a dumpling, some fried chicken meat balls, some omelette and some pieces of pumpkin.

"This is *tamagoyaki*," Yuki said, pointing at the omelette. "The broiled pumpkin is *kabocha no jikani*."

"Wow!" I said. It made my lunch look pretty average.

"What is your lunch?" Yuki asked.

I had a bread roll with cheese and salad. A muesli bar. Apple juice. And a mango.

"Wow!" said Yuki. (She picked up words really quickly.)

I looked at Yuki. My lunch didn't seem very special to me. "Wow what?" I said.

"In Japan," Yuki said, "mangoes are very, very expensive. They're sold packed in special boxes, just one mango to a box."

"What? Mangoes?" I said. "It's just from the tree in our backyard."

"I've never had a mango," Yuki said.

I looked at Yuki's obentoo. "Want to swap something?" I said.

So we did. I tried some *tamagoyaki*. Yuki showed me how to use the chopsticks. They were hard to handle. I kept dropping the omelette. But when I got some into my mouth, it tasted great.

Yuki tried the mango. I had to show her how to peel it. The juice ran down her chin, onto her hands, down her arms and dripped off her elbows.

"Yum!" we both said.

"You said you have a mango tree in your backyard?" said Yuki. "Has it got many mangoes?"

"It's loaded," I said. "Want to come and see it some time?"

Yuki did.

She's my best friend now. We share our obentoo every day.